Copyright © 2024 by Frederick Fichman.

All rights reserved. No part of this book, in its unique form, as developed and herein electronically-printed by Frederick Fichman, may be reproduced or utilized in any form or by any means, electronic or mechanical, including photocopying, recording or by any information storage and retrieval systems, without permission in writing from the publisher, except where permitted by law.

Electronically-Printed in the United States of America

All characters in this book are fictitious, and any resemblance to actual persons, living or dead, is purely coincidental.

Frederick Fichman
Marana, AZ 85658

fred@frederickfichman.com

Copyright, 2024

Introduction

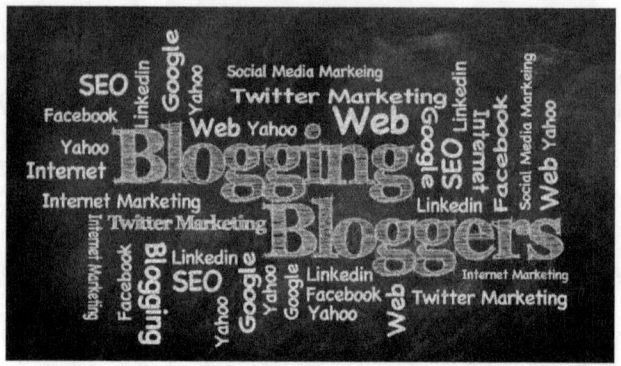

Welcome to **"How to Make Money Blogging in 2024 and Beyond."** If you're someone who loves to share their thoughts, ideas, and experiences through blogging and dreams of turning that passion into a lucrative side hustle or even a full-time career, you've come to the right place.

In this comprehensive guide, we'll explore the myriad opportunities available for bloggers to monetize their content and generate a steady stream of income. Whether you're a seasoned blogger looking to diversify your revenue streams or a newcomer eager to embark on your blogging journey, you'll find valuable insights and practical tips to help you succeed.

Blogging isn't just a hobby anymore; it's a bona fide small business idea with the potential to yield significant financial rewards. From driving product sales for your own brand to earning commissions from affiliate programs, the possibilities are endless.

Throughout this guide, we'll delve into 11 proven revenue streams utilized by professional bloggers who have mastered the art of monetizing their websites. But before we dive into the specifics, let's address a common question: How much money can bloggers really make?

The earning potential in the world of blogging is staggering. Established bloggers like Ryan Robinson and Adam Enfroy serve as shining examples, earning upwards of tens of thousands or even millions of dollars per month from their blogs.

However, it's essential to recognize that not every blogger will achieve such lofty heights of success. The income potential of your blog hinges on various factors, including your chosen niche and your monetization strategies.

In this guide, we'll explore how to identify a profitable niche that aligns with your interests and expertise, as well as delve into a range of monetization strategies, from building an email list and writing sponsored product reviews to selling advertising placements and offering digital products.

To be successful please remember the following:

Be Consistent With Your Blog Schedule

Write with Clarity

Imagination, Dazzle and Challenge Your Reader with Fascinating Content

Give Your Readers Content That is a Benefit to Them

Blog about What You Like, Know, and What Interests You

Explore, Discover, and have Fun

So, if you're ready to unlock the full earning potential of your blog and take your passion for writing to the next level, let's dive into the world of money-making blogging together. You can do this, you really can. Let's have some fun and make some money in the process.

Chapter One: Finding Your Profitable Niche

Choosing the right niche for your blog is crucial. It's the foundation upon which your entire blogging journey rests. But not all niches are created equal. In this chapter, we'll explore how to identify a profitable niche that aligns with your interests and expertise.

You'll come across bloggers thriving in diverse niches, ranging from business software to pet accessories. However, success isn't guaranteed in every niche. A profitable blog niche must meet three essential criteria:

1. Alignment with Your Skills and Interests: Your blog's content quality plays a pivotal role in attracting and retaining an audience. To consistently produce high-quality content, it's crucial

to choose a niche that you're passionate about or skilled in. Blogging about topics that genuinely interest you not only makes the process more enjoyable but also increases the likelihood of monetization. After all, it's easier to remain dedicated to something we love.

2. Assessing Competition: Analyze the competitive landscape of your chosen niche. The presence of established blogs, brands, or forums indicates that money can be made in that niche. Additionally, conduct a Google search to gauge keyword ranking difficulty. If prominent brands with significant marketing budgets dominate the search results, it might be challenging to drive organic traffic to your blog. Opting for a niche with lower competition increases your chances of standing out and attracting an audience.

3. Evaluating Monetization Potential: Consider the monetization opportunities available within your chosen niche. Are companies willing to pay for advertising space on similar blogs? Are there numerous affiliate programs offering products

relevant to your niche? These factors indicate the potential profitability of your chosen niche. A niche with clear monetization potential sets the stage for sustainable income generation from your blog.

By carefully considering these criteria, you can pinpoint a profitable niche that aligns with your interests, skills, and revenue goals. This sets the stage for building a successful blog with a dedicated following and ample monetization opportunities.

Chapter 2: Building Your Email List

In the world of blogging, having a loyal audience is key to monetizing your efforts effectively. But how do you cultivate such a following? One powerful method is through the strategic building of an email list. In this chapter, we'll explore why an email list is invaluable for bloggers and how to construct one that nurtures relationships and drives revenue.

When someone subscribes to your email list, they're granting you access to one of the most personal spaces in their digital lives—their inbox. This direct line of communication allows you to engage with your audience on a deeper level and establish trust over time. As Brittany Berger, founder of Work Brighter, attests, email marketing often proves to be the most lucrative sales channel for bloggers.

To entice visitors to sign up for your mailing list, it's essential to offer valuable incentives. Consider providing free resources such as checklists, curated lists of recommended products, or blog content packaged in downloadable PDFs. These incentives not only encourage sign-ups but also set the stage for ongoing engagement.

Once you've captured their attention and secured their email address, the real work begins. Nurturing your email list involves delivering consistently high-quality content that educates, entertains, and resonates with your subscribers. By providing value through your emails, you'll cultivate a loyal audience primed to act on your recommendations.

Lily Ugbaja, creator of FindingBalance.Mom, exemplifies the power of leveraging an email list to drive revenue. In just two weeks, Lily turned her blog into a profitable venture by strategically promoting her products and relevant affiliate offerings to her subscribers. By employing tactics like tripwires and utilizing lead magnets to incentivize sign-ups, Lily transformed her modest monthly page views into a lucrative income stream.

Moreover, monetizing your email list doesn't stop at promotional emails. Many bloggers successfully charge subscribers for access to exclusive content through monthly subscription fees. Platforms like Substack provide an avenue for publishing premium content directly to your audience while generating revenue through subscriptions.

In summary, building and nurturing an email list is a cornerstone of successful blogging. By providing value, fostering engagement, and strategically monetizing your subscriber base, you can transform your blog into a thriving business venture, just like Lily and countless other bloggers have done.

Chapter Three: Ethical Considerations in Writing Sponsored Product Reviews

In the digital marketplace, businesses strive to garner social proof that validates the value of their products. One effective avenue for achieving this is through sponsored product reviews, where bloggers are compensated to share their opinions with their audience.

To initiate this monetization strategy, reach out to brands aligned with your niche and propose the idea of sponsoring a review on your blog. If you already use the product in question, the process essentially incurs no additional cost, as you're simply sharing your genuine opinion with your audience while being compensated for your time and expertise.

However, it's crucial to navigate this terrain with caution. Recent incidents, such as Fashion Nova's $4.2 million fine by the Federal Trade Commission (FTC) for suppressing negative reviews, underscore the importance of transparency and integrity in sponsored content.

The FTC has established guidelines that govern sponsored content, emphasizing the need for full disclosure regarding any incentives or compensation received. To avoid potential legal repercussions and maintain trust with your audience, it's imperative to include a clear disclaimer at the outset of your review, explicitly stating any financial arrangements: "I've been compensated to write this review, and may receive a commission if you purchase this product."

Moreover, prioritize honesty and authenticity in your reviews by presenting a balanced assessment that encompasses both the positive and negative aspects of the product. In an era where consumers value transparency and authenticity, adopting a candid approach can foster credibility and trust with your audience, thereby enhancing the effectiveness of your sponsored content.

In summary, while sponsored product reviews offer a valuable monetization opportunity for bloggers, ethical considerations should remain paramount. By adhering to FTC guidelines, maintaining transparency, and providing honest evaluations, you can navigate this landscape responsibly, ensuring both legal compliance and the preservation of your audience's trust and confidence in your recommendations.

Chapter 4: Maximizing Revenue Through Advertising Placements

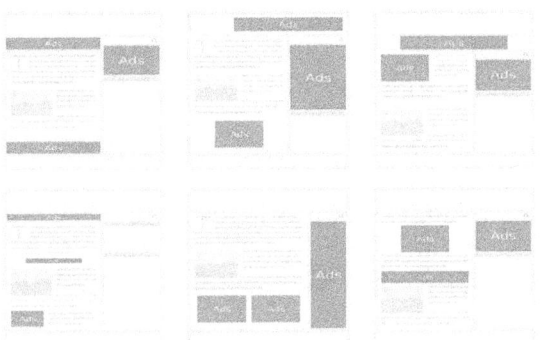

In the ever-evolving landscape of digital marketing, companies are eager to leverage bloggers' platforms to promote their products and services. Selling advertising placements on your blog presents a lucrative opportunity to monetize otherwise unused space and generate a steady stream of income. In this chapter, we'll explore two distinct approaches to selling advertising placements and uncover strategies for maximizing your earnings in this revenue stream.

1. Negotiating Directly with Companies: For bloggers seeking maximum control and potential for higher earnings, negotiating directly with companies is a viable option. This approach involves identifying

businesses within your niche and pitching them on the benefits of advertising on your blog. While this method may require significant time and strong negotiation skills, the payoff can be substantial in terms of revenue.

2. Utilizing Advertising Networks: Alternatively, bloggers can opt for a more hands-off approach by partnering with advertising networks such as Google AdSense, Mediavine, or Raptive (formerly AdThrive). These platforms streamline the process by claiming ad space on your blog and handling advertiser billing. By simply embedding the provided code on your site, you can start earning revenue from displayed ads with minimal effort.

Emily Brookes, a successful blogger at Emily May, attests to the profitability of display ads, which comprise a significant portion of her blog's revenue stream. Display ads offer consistent income month after month, making them an attractive option for bloggers seeking passive income opportunities.

To maximize revenue from advertising placements, driving website traffic becomes paramount. Ad networks typically pay per 1,000 impressions (CPM), with average rates hovering around $1.25. Therefore, increasing your blog's exposure to a larger audience directly correlates to higher earnings from ad placements.

While some ad networks impose minimum page-view requirements for eligibility, investing time and effort to meet these thresholds can yield significant dividends in the long run. Monica Lent, founder of Not a Nomad Blog, highlights the substantial revenue potential of this type of blog advertising.

Afoma Umesi, the creator behind Reading Middle Grade, underscores the value of ads as a passive income stream. Despite starting her blog as a hobby, Afoma turned to ads and affiliate links to monetize her platform effectively. With a focus on providing value to her audience, she demonstrates how ads can seamlessly integrate into a blog while generating substantial revenue.

In conclusion, selling advertising placements on your blog offers a reliable avenue for monetization, whether through direct negotiations with companies or partnership with advertising networks. By prioritizing website traffic and leveraging advertising platforms strategically, you can unlock the full earning potential of your blog while providing value to your audience.

Chapter 5: Affiliate Marketing

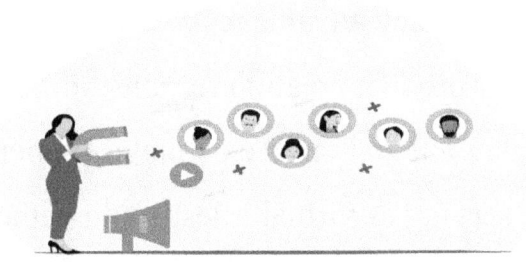

Harnessing the Power of Affiliate MarketingAffiliate marketing stands as a cornerstone of monetization for bloggers, offering a seamless way to recommend products to your audience while earning commissions for each sale made through your unique referral links. In this chapter, we'll delve into the intricacies of affiliate marketing, exploring its revenue potential and strategies for success.

At its core, affiliate marketing involves promoting products or services to your blog's audience and earning a commission for each sale generated through your referral link. This presents a lucrative revenue opportunity for bloggers, as the content they share naturally influences their audience's purchasing decisions. By positioning your blog as a source of valuable educational content, you can foster the trust and credibility needed to drive conversions.

One of the key advantages of affiliate marketing is the absence of product creation responsibilities. Bloggers can seamlessly integrate into existing ecommerce businesses, serving as virtual salespeople without the hassle of managing inventory, shipping logistics, or customer service inquiries.

To begin monetizing your blog through affiliate marketing, it's essential to join reputable affiliate networks such as ShareASale or ClickBank. These platforms offer a diverse array of affiliate programs spanning various industries, allowing bloggers to align with products and services relevant to their niche. Upon joining a program, you'll gain access to custom affiliate links and comprehensive dashboards to track your affiliate revenue.

Additionally, bloggers can explore high-ticket affiliate programs offered by merchants selling premium products like electronics, jewelry, or software. Recommending such products to your audience can result in substantial commission payouts, providing bloggers with a lucrative revenue stream. For instance, Shopify affiliates earn generous commissions on subscription plan referrals, further highlighting the potential of high-ticket affiliate partnerships.

In summary, affiliate marketing presents bloggers with a powerful means of monetizing their platforms without the need to create their own products. By strategically selecting affiliate programs, crafting compelling content, and fostering trust with your audience, you can unlock the full earning potential of affiliate marketing while delivering value to your readers.

Chapter 6: Monetizing Your Expertise Through Services

As your blog gains momentum and your audience expands, you naturally become synonymous with the topics you cover. This association not only boosts your credibility but also positions you as an authority—a quality highly sought after by those seeking specialized services. In this chapter, we'll explore how leveraging your expertise to offer services can be a lucrative avenue for monetizing your blog.

Mushfiq, the visionary behind The Website Flip, emphasizes the revenue potential of consulting, particularly in the B2B sector. Harnessing the trust and interest of your audience, consulting can serve as a high-yield, low-commitment method of monetizing your blog. By identifying areas where your knowledge can benefit others, you can provide valuable insights and guidance while earning a substantial income.

While managing a service-oriented business demands time and effort, it can swiftly translate into online earnings. By leveraging your blog content to showcase your expertise, you can command higher rates and attract premium clients seeking your specialized skills.

Examples of services you can offer in tandem with your blog include:

- Consulting services
- Graphic design
- Freelance writing
- Virtual assistance
- Classes or workshops

To streamline your workflow and enhance client experience, consider integrating scheduling and payment platforms like Acuity and Calendly. These tools not only save time but also facilitate seamless communication and transaction management.

Promoting your services through your blog can be achieved through various methods, such as creating dedicated landing pages or featuring display ads. By leveraging your blog's reach and credibility, you can attract new clients and expand your service-based business.

In conclusion, offering services presents an invaluable opportunity for bloggers to monetize their expertise while providing tangible value to their audience. By leveraging your authority, utilizing efficient tools, and strategically promoting your services through your blog, you can establish a thriving service-oriented venture while continuing to engage and grow your audience.

Chapter 7: Unleashing the Potential of Selling Digital Products

In the realm of monetizing your blog, selling digital products stands out as a scalable and lucrative option. Unlike service-based businesses, where your income is tied to the hours you invest, and unlike physical products, with their associated shipping and manufacturing costs, digital products offer a streamlined and efficient way to generate revenue. In this chapter, we'll explore how you can leverage digital products to maximize your blog's earning potential.

Dylan Houlihan, the visionary behind Swift Salary, recognized the value of diversifying income streams and gaining greater control over his earnings by adding digital products to his portfolio. By creating digital products once, you can sell them infinitely through your blog—a concept often referred to as "build once, sell twice." Dylan's experience highlights the potential of digital products to provide a steady stream of income with minimal ongoing effort.

To identify which digital products will resonate with your audience, consider conducting a reader survey to uncover unmet needs or challenges. Armed with this insight, you can develop digital products tailored to address specific pain points, such as:

- Ebooks
- Printables
- Workbooks
- Online courses

Benjamin Houy, the driving force behind French Together, has successfully integrated digital products into his blog's monetization strategy, with a French course accounting for a significant portion of revenue. Benjamin emphasizes that creating a product tailored to your audience's needs is key to success. Your digital product doesn't have to be perfect at launch; it simply needs to

provide genuine value and meet your audience's expectations.

Selling your own digital product offers numerous advantages, including the ability to refine and improve based on customer feedback. Unlike affiliate programs or ad revenue, where external factors can impact earnings, selling digital products puts you in control of your income stream. Additionally, you're not reliant on third-party platforms, mitigating the risk of program discontinuation or ad blockers impacting revenue.

In summary, selling digital products presents bloggers with a scalable and profitable means of monetizing their expertise and providing value to their audience. By identifying audience needs, creating compelling products, and continually refining based on feedback, you can unlock the full earning potential of digital product sales while retaining control over your revenue stream.

Chapter 8: Capitalizing on Your Blog's Influence to Sell Physical Products

If your blog boasts a dedicated following, tapping into the enthusiasm of your loyal readers can not only strengthen their connection with your brand but also serve as a lucrative revenue stream. Selling physical products allows you to leverage your blog's influence to provide tangible goods that resonate with your audience. In this chapter, we'll explore how you can harness the power of your blog to sell physical products and generate income while fostering a deeper connection with your audience.

The print-on-demand model emerges as an ideal solution for small blogging businesses, offering the flexibility to produce merchandise without the burden of excess inventory or upfront costs. Platforms like Printful or Printify empower bloggers to create custom merchandise tailored to their audience's preferences, including items such as mugs, t-shirts, stickers, posters, tote bags, and phone cases. By leveraging these services, you can offer branded merchandise that resonates with your audience and reinforces their connection with your blog.

For those seeking a more hands-on approach, launching your own online store provides a platform to showcase your products and engage directly with your audience. Treat your blog's readership as your initial customer base, leveraging your existing relationship to drive sales and foster loyalty.

Richard Belton, the mastermind behind Kaito Ridge, transitioned from relying on Amazon affiliate commissions to taking control of his blog's income by launching a Shopify store. By diversifying his monetization strategy and offering physical products related to his niche, Richard tapped into the enthusiasm of his audience and created a new revenue stream for his blog.

In summary, selling physical products offers bloggers a powerful means of monetizing their influence and providing value to their audience. By leveraging print-on-demand services or launching your own online store, you can transform your blog into a thriving ecommerce platform while strengthening your connection with your readership.

Chapter 9: Cultivating a Membership Community

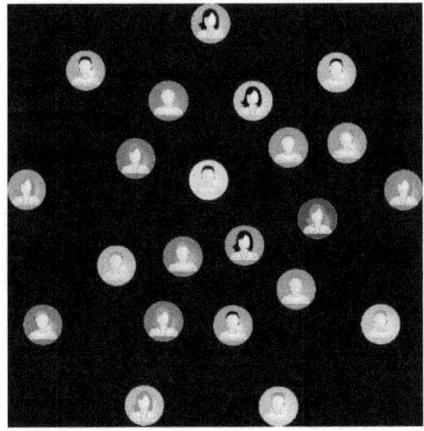

Elevate the experience for your most dedicated readers by inviting them into a VIP community, where they can access exclusive content and benefits in exchange for a modest fee. Establishing a membership community not only fosters a sense of belonging but also taps into the growing importance of social connection in an increasingly digital world. Research indicates that communities not only contribute to improved mental well-being but also drive consumer loyalty, with over half of shoppers willing to spend more on brands that share their values.

Michael Keenan, the driving force behind the Peak Freelance blog, attests to the value of creating a membership program to sustain blogging efforts. By offering exclusive content, special offers, and even dedicated communication channels like Slack, Keenan provides members with a premium experience tailored to their needs and interests.

When structuring your membership program, consider offering flexible payment options, such as monthly or yearly subscriptions, with a slight discount for annual commitments. This not only ensures a consistent revenue stream but also incentivizes long-term engagement and investment from your community members.

Chapter 10: Leveraging YouTube for Additional Revenue Streams

Unlock the full potential of your blog content by extending your reach to YouTube and tapping into its monetization opportunities. In this chapter, we'll explore how integrating video marketing into your blogging strategy can not only enhance affiliate commission earnings but also open new revenue streams through YouTube's monetization features.

Did you know that 88% of people have been influenced to make a purchase after watching a branded video? By incorporating video tutorials, reviews, or hauls into your content repertoire, you can leverage the power of visual storytelling to drive conversions and earn rewards when viewers make purchases based on your recommendations.

To maximize your earnings, approach each piece of content as the foundation for a video script. Record yourself discussing the same topic covered in your blog post, then edit and upload the video to YouTube. This approach allows you to cater to different audience preferences and expand your reach across platforms.

A prime example of this strategy in action is A Beautiful Mess, whose bloggers created a YouTube video demonstrating how to build built-in shelves. The video directs viewers to the corresponding blog post, which contains affiliate links to the products featured in the tutorial. By integrating video content with their blog, A Beautiful Mess effectively expands their audience reach and revenue potential.

There are several reasons why incorporating YouTube into your monetization strategy is advantageous. Firstly, not everyone prefers written content—some prefer consuming information through videos. By diversifying your content offerings, you can cater to varying audience preferences and capture a wider audience base.

Secondly, sharing content on both Google and YouTube increases the likelihood of your target audience discovering your content. With Google and YouTube being the two most popular search engines globally, leveraging both platforms enhances your content's visibility and accessibility, ultimately driving affiliate sales and revenue.

Moreover, an active YouTube channel opens additional revenue opportunities through the YouTube Partner program. Once you surpass 1,000 subscribers and 4,000 watch hours, you can enroll in the program and monetize your videos through advertisements displayed before your content. This supplementary income stream complements your blog earnings and enhances your overall revenue potential.

In conclusion, integrating YouTube into your blogging strategy offers a myriad of benefits, from expanding your audience reach to unlocking additional revenue streams. By leveraging video marketing and YouTube's monetization features, you can maximize your earning potential while providing valuable content to your audience across platforms.

By reinvesting membership fees into developing new content and products, you can continuously enhance the value proposition for your members while driving growth and sustainability for your blog.

In summary, establishing a membership community offers bloggers an opportunity to deepen their engagement with their audience and generate sustainable revenue. By offering exclusive benefits and fostering a sense of belonging, you can create a premium experience that resonates with your most dedicated readers, driving loyalty and long-term success for your blog.

Chapter 11: Harnessing the Power of Podcasting for Profit

In the digital landscape of 2024, podcasts have emerged as a powerhouse medium, with an estimated 100 million US citizens tuning in. However, podcasts are more than just a way to pass the time during morning commutes—they're a powerful tool for driving brand engagement and sparking conversations. Studies reveal that 70% of listeners visit a brand's website after hearing about its products through podcast sponsorships, while another 67% discuss the products with friends, making podcasts an enticing proposition for brands seeking to expand their reach.

Seize the opportunity to captivate your audience by creating your own podcast. Record engaging discussions on topics within your niche and distribute each episode across streaming platforms like Apple Podcasts or Spotify. By leveraging the intimacy and accessibility of podcasts, you can forge deeper connections with your audience and position yourself as a trusted voice within your industry.

Explore sponsorship opportunities by reaching out to brands aligned with your niche. Offer ad space within your podcast episodes, providing companies with a direct route to their target audience in exchange for a sponsorship fee. Utilize resources like a podcast revenue calculator to estimate potential earnings based on factors such as episode downloads and ad placements.

While podcasting presents a lucrative revenue stream, it also comes with its challenges. Building a loyal audience takes time and dedication and investing in quality equipment—such as a high-quality microphone and editing software—is essential for producing professional-grade content. However, with careful planning and execution, podcasting can become a valuable addition to your blogging business, offering a new avenue for revenue generation and audience engagement.

In summary, podcasting represents a dynamic opportunity to amplify your blog's reach and revenue potential. By harnessing the power of audio storytelling and securing sponsorships, you can create compelling content that resonates with your audience while generating income for your blogging endeavors.

Conclusion: Transforming Your Blog into a Profitable Venture

The journey to making money through blogging is as diverse as the individuals who embark upon it. While some may see immediate returns, for many, it's a gradual process that requires patience, persistence, and strategic experimentation.

Consider Brittany Berger, the founder of Work Brighter, who swiftly earned her first $100 online by offering a simple digital download to her early audience. Berger's proactive approach highlights the potential for quick wins in the blogging sphere, emphasizing the importance of seizing opportunities and embracing experimentation, even with a modest audience.

However, the timeline for achieving substantial income varies from blogger to blogger. For some, it may be a gradual progression, while others may experience rapid success. The key lies in building exceptional content and fostering a loyal readership, laying the foundation for successful monetization endeavors.

As you embark on your blogging journey, remember that there's no one-size-fits-all approach to turning your blog into a money-making machine. Experiment with different monetization tactics, leverage your unique strengths, niche expertise, and prioritize building meaningful connections with your audience.

In the realm of blogging, there's no shortage of opportunities to generate income. Whether through display advertising, affiliate marketing, or creating digital products, the possibilities are vast. By honing your skills, nurturing your audience, and staying committed to your vision, you can turn your blog into a lucrative venture that not only fulfills your financial goals but also brings value to your readers.

As you navigate the world of blogging and monetization, keep these guiding principles in mind, and remember that success is within reach for those who are willing to invest the time, effort, and creativity required to make their blogging dreams a reality.

HOT LIST: 15 Actions to Take After You Start Your Blog

1. **Share New Blog Post, every post, on Twitter**
2. **Share New Blog Post, every post, on Your Facebook Page or Group**
3. **Share New Blog Post, every post, on your Instagram**
4. **Share New Blog Post, every pin, on your Pinterest**
5. **Share New Blog Post, every post, for your E-Mail Subscribers**
6. **Share New Blog Post, every post, if they let you, on Similar Blogs or Sites**
7. **Share New Blog Post, every post, with photos on Photo Sharing Websites or FB groups**
8. **Share New Blog Post, every post, to Roundups (other sites looking for similar topics)**
9. **Make Sure Your New Blog Post is SEO Optimized. How to do that? Do a Google Search**
10. **Make Sure You Add Links and Mentions About Your Previous Posts**
11. **Make Sure You Keep a Content Calendar for Future Blogs, Keeps You On Track and Producing**
12. **Make Sure You Answers all Questions Through Your Email Accounts**
13. **Make Sure You Constantly Check Your Performance Analytics**

14. **Make Sure You Read, Learn, and Expand Your Knowledge on Your Topic**
15. **Make Sure You are Consistent, Week to Week, Keep Writing and Keep Producing**

Finally, why Blog? Because you have to and because you are compelled to. You are curious and inquisitive. You are interested to the point of obsession with your topic. You want to be heard and you want to make some money off your efforts.

And believe me, I know, once you're hooked there is no going back. You'll find blogging is now part of your life, making you money and having a helluva lot of fun.

So, hit the Start button.

Thanks for reading and sticking with me.

The End

www.ingramcontent.com/pod-product-compliance
Lightning Source LLC
Chambersburg PA
CBHW050248230526
45470CB00005B/2159